GLORIA MONTERO'S

FRIDA K.

...*Frida K.* may prove to be one of the most important works of both feminist and solo theatre. CANADIAN THEATRE ENCYCLOPEDIA

...an epic poem for one, creating a voice palpable with reality. VILLAGE VOICE

...complex, haunting, nasty, grasping, passionate and, above all, immensely alive. VARIETY

...a wonderful play...absolutely rivetting... astounding...CBC (Toronto)

GLORIA MONTERO

Novelist, playwright, poet Gloria Montero grew up in Australia in a family of Spanish immigrants. After studies in theatre and music, she began to work in radio and theatre then moved to Canada where she continued her career as writer, broadcaster, scriptwriter and producer of radio and film documentaries. She now lives in Barcelona where she has continued to write and publish. Her plays have been performed in countries around the world.

www.gloriamontero.com

FRIDA K.

GLORIA MONTERO

Sesata World Editions

Frida K.

Sesata World Editions

Copyright © Gloria Montero 1995

The purchase of this book in no way gives the purchaser the right to perform the play in public, either in a staged production or a reading. All applications for public performance should be addressed to the playwright: Gloria Montero, C/- The Writers' Union of Canada, 90 Richmond Street East, Suite 200, Toronto ON MSC 1P1, Canada.
e-mail: info@writersunion.ca.

Front cover and theatrical photographs used in this book: **Allegra Fulton** as Frida in National Arts Centre production of *Frida K.*, Ottawa, Canada (2007). Photos: © Andrée Lanthier (Lanthier Photo). The photo on page 35 from the Tarragon Theatre, Toronto, production is by Michael Cooper.

Author photo: Pilar Aymerich

Cover design and layout: Sanzsoto

For Allegra,
and for Roser Bru
who introduced me to Frida
many years ago.

I want to make some difference to this world, just by being here.

—Frida Kahlo

The play in three movements preceded by Frida's Dream runs approximately 1 hour 20 minutes with no intermission.

The set and stage directions indicated throughout the script are those that were used in the first full production of FRIDA K. November 9 - December 10, 1995, at the Tarragon Theatre, Toronto, Canada, directed by Peter Hinton with Allegra Fulton as Frida. Set and costumes were by Ken Garnhum, lighting by Bonnie Beecher and sound design by Naomi Campbell.

FRIDA K.

FRIDA'S DREAM: *A spotlight illuminates the figure of FRIDA which appears to float in space. She wears a red scarf on her head and her arm is raised with a clenched fist. She speaks into a microphone as if addressing a political rally.*

FRIDA

I was a cashier in a pharmacy...a book-keeper in a lumber yard. I learnt typing and shorthand and became a librarian. The nice lady that hired me made sure she made use of me for everything.

(Saucily) E-ve-ry-thing! I worked in a factory until an engraver friend of my father's gave me a job copying prints.

I've always done what had to be done. I put down on canvas what I can see around me.

We gotta wake people up...make'em realize that we gotta change things. That's what the revolution is about. And this country needs changing...**que verguenza!** Everything Mexican, especially the Indians, is treated like shit. If we're not careful we'll end up with all our natural resources in foreign hands!

Being Mexican is something I am proud of! I am the most Mexican of my father's children because I came in with the revolution. Eight-thirty in the morning, July 7th, 1910. My mother could hear the first shots being fired when my head popped out! Pam! Pam!

It rained like hell the day I was born...the Gods were crying because they knew what was gonna happen.

My mother's milk dried up after my birth and they had to find me an Indian nana. My father told me how they used to wash her big, dark, swollen breasts every time I had to feed. Top quality 100% pure Mexican milk!

Here I am a little angel in my wooden cradle with

my good Christian names—Magdalena Carmen —but it's my third name that's the real one. Frida...it means peace in German. Peace!

At the word "peace" crazy mocking laughter—the laughter of a dummy in a fun fair— echoes around the set as the spotlight dims leaving the stage in darkness.

MOVEMENT ONE

THE BLUE HOUSE:
FRIDA's bedroom/studio with her four-poster bed complete with its Judas figure of Death. Upstage centre are double doors.

The set, however, must suggest more than a mere living area. Death in various guises, along with elements of Frida's life and paintings, add a surreal quality to the stage on which she will confront not only her own end but the vision of herself that will be left for posterity. Key elements include a dressing table on which stands a vase of tall white arum lilies, a skeleton hanging on the wall, a blue wardrobe, a mirror, an easel, an image of the Virgin of Guadalupe, a watermelon, as well as canvases, medicines, crutches and metal corsets. Cigarettes and bottles of pulque, brandy and tequila are at hand as Frida drinks and smokes heavily during the play.

FRIDA is in constant pain. Specific indications of pain in the text are where she can no longer handle it.

FRIDA (off)

Diego! Diego? **Hijo de la chingada madre!** How long Have I been asleep?

FRIDA enters in a wheelchair.

Where are you? You can't fool me, I could find you with my eyes shut. Hey, don't play games with me, **Dieguito**. Not today. It's my big day, remember. I'm getting to be pretty big bananas myself, you know.

Cielito, is that you? Who is it? Who's there?

FRIDA turns to the audience.

Oh, it's only you!

Diego...darling...**Dieguito**? Where the hell are you?

She finds a note attached to the door-frame.

'**Mi Friduchita, amorcita de mi vida**, I've got some business to do, but I'll meet you later at the gallery. Everyone's gonna be there so get yourself together my pretty little **Mejicana.**'

She snorts.

And he sends me fuc-bulous lilies!

Pause

(Bowing formally) Doña Carmen de Rivera!

That's how Diego used to introduce me when Hitler was in power. He was doing it to protect me, but I didn't like it. It was like saying that all Germans were Nazis...**incluso mi papa**!

FRIDA goes to make a mock Nazi salute but pulls her hand down.

(Cheekily) Oooh...tsk-tsk.

> *Pleased with the reaction to her impertinence, FRIDA begins to swagger impudently.*

Hi there, folks, I'm from the Los Angeles Times. Now the news we have in the States is that this here Frida Kahlo is one hell of a painter...and one goddamn hell of a lay! Now where the fuck is she?

And Sr. Rivera, exactly where the hell did he get to? He's pushing me to cut off my hair again! Last time I did that, he went crazy! But it was easier to take the scissors to my hair than what I really felt like cutting off right then!

Business to do! I bet he did! Probably gone with one his models or some little English teacher from Chattanooga. He'll be telling her what a great guy he is...how he fought the revolution. Maybe he'll even show her his gun. Ooh, he's never without his gun. Tonight, even at my show, everybody looking at my paintings, he'll tell me how he wiggled his hand between her thighs and bit on her tits till she begged him to stop.

Take that look off your face, lady. That's what's wrong

with you, you're a prude...an old-fashioned prig! You never liked Diego. You think I should've...Ah, what the hell do I care what you think. You'll never understand.

Diego is like the underside of my own soul. That guy needs me. He can't live without me. Heloise and Abelard...Dante and Beatriz...Diego and Frida!

She sees herself in the mirror.

Ufff! Frida, **la fantasma!** Wouldn't that give 'em something to sink their teeth into?

Yeah, well...you've got to excuse me but I've gotta get myself together. Diego will be waiting for me at the gallery.

FRIDA washes down a handful of pills from her medicines with a tumblerful of brandy. She peers at herself in the mirror and speaks directly to the skeleton.

At least, **Pelona**, I've still got hair! That's more than you can say!

*Cackling wildly FRIDA begins
her elaborate hair-do.*

So everybody's gonna be there, eh? Half of them probably think I'm not even gonna make it myself. Even **mis doctorcitos** don't want me to go. 'It'll be too much for you, **cariño**. In any case, there'll be enough Fridas in the gallery with your paintings on the walls.' What do they know? What does anybody know? Not go to my own exhibition? Fat chance I'd miss a great show like that!

Diego says my name's spread right across the gallery windows in big red letters. Frankly, I never expected anything like that. I never imagined the inside of my guts would mean much to anyone else.

Though the first show I ever had—that big show in New York—I sold everything...that was the turning point. Then when Breton came he said I just had to go to Paris...he would arrange a big show for me.

Paris! People talk about Paris like it's Mars or Venus. The Tour Eiffel...le Seine...Nôtre Dame! Frankly, I kept looking for the Hunchback up there in the rafters. Old Quasimodo and I might understand each other...but no one in Paris talked my language. Marcel Duchamp is the only one of all that bunch of cuckoo lunatic sons of bitches with his feet on the ground. He found someone who agreed to show my work though there were only two paintings they'd exhibit. The rest were too 'shocking'! Can you believe it?

Well, I suppose you can...but it doesn't make sense. There is Dali with his soft floppy dicks all over the place, and me and my little curled-up foetuses are too much for them!

All I wanted was to get out of France before I went nuts myself. It was a helluva time! Over the border Franco'd just named himself **caudillo** and the French were actually putting Spanish refugees in concentration camps. It's hard to believe...all those fat-arsed democracies of Europe refusing to look fascism in the eye and they call it Non-Intervention! With Diego's help I managed to get four hundred Spaniards on a ship to Mexico.

I knew they'd be safe here. Thank God, I met Picasso...he is a real person. Not like the rest of those intellectual bastards warming their **culitos** in cafés talking about "culture" and "art" and "revolution" and they don't do a damn thing about any of it! I taught Picasso a couple of things... *(She grins mischievously)*...and he taught me things as well!

(Sings)
**Los cuatro generales,
los cuatro generales,
los cuatro generales,
Mamita mia, que se han alzado,
que se han alzado.**

**El de la mula torda,
El de la mula torda,
El de la mula torda,
Mamita mia, es mi marido,
Es mi marido.**

The part of Paris I liked best was the dancing. I went dancing every night...tangos, pasodobles, fox-trots! *(Pain)* Yeah...well, for the most of six weeks I sat around on my bum waiting. But when the show finally opened...*(Pain)* Aieee! I took Paris by storm!

The Louvre bought one of my paintings...not even Diego can say that. Surrealism from the New World they call it...they don't understand anything!

I don't have to dream up a damn thing—it's all laid out in technicolour just waiting to be copied! Not that it makes much difference. Here in Mexico no one gives a goddamn what the big **cacas** in Paris think about me. Here I am still just little Frida de Rivera ...**y punto.**

Tonight is the first time anyone here thought I was worth a show of my own. Why has it taken them so long to accept me?

> *FRIDA begins applying her makeup.*

In Mexico you're nobody unless the government has asked you to paint history on their goddamn walls where everybody can see it!

Of course here, we needed ten years of revolution before we could paint our history the way it really happened. Diego, he was the first to understand. He saw the power of the Mayan frescos in Chiapas and Yucatan and he knew you liberate people just showing them their true history.

Ten years to give Mexico back to los **Mejicanos!** And then people stopped having to powder their skin to make it lighter or persuade themselves that their grandfather or at least their great-grandmother had been Spanish.

Being Mexican became something to be proud of!

Ten years! It was a terrible time for a photographer like papa. The only pictures worth having were scenes of your own dinner-table with enough food for the whole family.

But we managed...because my mother was practical. Practical...and hysterical about religion. We prayed and prayed and prayed all the time. It drove my father crazy.

'Their bellies are empty yet they kneel down in churches where the statues are made of gold! Our streets look like the Champs-Élysées with buildings on them like decorated birthday cakes. They want pretty pictures, Frida...delicate colours, the light all soft and gentle. Nothing really Mexican at all.' That's what we got for bedtime stories! My baby sister Cristi and me, we used to hide in this wardrobe and yell our little lungs out...all the revolutionary songs we'd heard at the market. Then mama would come in and insist we pray to Our Lady, the immaculate bloody Virgin!

Está bien! We had our revolution all right. And when it was over Papa was determined I was gonna go to the most progressive school in the whole country. He'd made up his mind...I was going to become Doktor Frida Kahlo!

FRIDA K.

*She has a spasm of pain
then laughs, lifting herself
out of the wheelchair.*

Well, you gotta admit I learned about medicine all right...but in my own way. What I learned at school was about Marx—Marx and Rivera!

*It is the schoolgirl FRIDA
who talks now.*

Diego is famous...and fat, fantastically fat! He works up there on the scaffold dressed in his big baggy clothes that always looks as if he's slept in them for at least one week. He wears a big cowboy hat, clumsy black miner's boots about this size, and a wide leather belt around his hips...with bullets in it, of course, for his gun! He's like a...a big fat toad pulsing with energy. You sense him thinking something, then you see it come right out of him, out through his arm onto the wall.

I've never seen pure energy like that before. He is like a God up there...one of our ancient Mexican gods. Though he acts human enough. That guy'll do it anywhere! Wanna bet? Is he making out with his wife Lupe or one of his little **modelitos?**

Pause

I put soap on the stairs down from the platform where he is working and then I hide and I wait for him to come down and fall. **Jo!** He's so slow and heavy...he doesn't even notice. Lupe found me that day. She probably thought I was his mistress or something. Who knows? I certainly considered it. I even told my friends...one day I was going to have Diego Rivera's baby! The big fat frog's baby!

FRIDA laughs bitterly.

But can you believe it, I was already in love...madly in love with Alex, **mi compañero Alex, divertido y guapo!** We were the children of the revolution. Nothing was out of bounds to us. We were gonna conquer the world! We talked about it all the time...the Golden Gate Bridge...Berlin...Venice...the lights...the bars!

I was so impatient to live. I could see my whole life stretching out before me and it didn't seem anything could ever go wrong. I hadn't learned yet about the Virgin and the power she wields. To tell you the truth, I underestimated her.

A trolley car can be heard.

It was Mary who did me in, you know. The Virgin of Guadalupe herself! I was raped before her very eyes and she didn't do a damn thing to help me. She just stood there, swaying like a gypsy, her eyes wide open while that fucking rod—steel-hard and insistent—thrust right up the middle of me almost parting me in two.

All at once I grew old. From one moment to the other I learned everything there was to know! I was like Papa's Doktor Faustus...but in reverse. He sold his soul to the devil to stay young forever. But I was only seventeen years old. My soul had been sold without my permission.

Pause

Mi queridisimo Alex, why don't you come to see me? Don't be worried about what's happened. I'll be your "older woman", an experienced older woman can be pretty hot stuff for a young man! I'll teach you things you've never even dreamed about! Why don't you answer my letters? I've heard your parents are sending you to Europe. All those times we dreamed about going away together and now you are going to Berlin, to Florence and Paris and I am here alone in bed, trapped in this iron cast that makes my body burn as if one million devils are lighting fires inside of me! My body is in flames but I am bitterly cold. They've thrown me away and left me here alone.

Don't go...please don't abandon me!

She picks up her diary and attempts to draw.

Now I paint what I see. I paint and paint and paint. It's like a drug for me, the only drug that works. The tips of my nerves are like radar. I can see things beyond my own skin the way I've seen inside beetles and butterflies under my father's microscope. My own pain is alive and raw but now I can see and feel all the anguish inside everyone else as well—all the confusion, the hurt, the fear. Oh, Alex! Alex!

MOVEMENT TWO

There is a knock at the door.

MALE SERVANT (off)

Señorita Frida. ¿Estás bien? Necesitas ayuda? Ya es tarde. Tienes que irte.

FRIDA

Metiche! Por el amor de Dios, déjame en paz. Estoy vistiéndome.

MALE SERVANT (off)

Como quieras. Pero aqui estoy si no puedes sola.

FRIDA

If I am going to live at all I have to do it on my own terms. I want to make some difference to this world just by being here.

She removes her blouse to reveal a painted plaster corset. After swallowing a long shot of brandy, she lifts herself out of her wheelchair and strides across the stage.

FRIDA laughs as she remembers back.

Hey there, Rivera. **Señor** Rivera, please come down for a minute...I've got something I want to discuss with you. Yeah, it's me calling. Please...it's very important.

Cut it out! I didn't come here for fun! I want you to look at these paintings and tell me what you think of them. Are they any good? I need you to level with me. If you don't think they're worth a shit then tell me. I'll get a job doing something else. I gotta earn some money to help my parents.

You really think so? Listen, I've got a whole stack of other canvases at home. Will you come and see them?

Pause

This is the bed where Diego and I first made love. I've done everything in this bed. I've spent half my life in it...it's like a part of me. When we went to the States, the first time, it was my bed I missed most of all.

She lights a cigarette.

One night Diego and I we are at some rich biddy's mansion in Manhattan. It's a goddamn palace—cathedral ceilings, chandeliers like diamonds, gold frames like chocolate wrapping around the paintings on the walls. Diego's going on about the revolution like he fought it himself. And all around the table I am looking at the pink and white boobs in satin dresses panting up and down, up and down, as Diego gives them the business about Pancho Villa and Zapata.

My English was not so good yet...but what the hell!

(FRIDA addresses the crowd at the dinner party)
Joder! My bed was a battlefield of the revolution! One day I was lying there in my bed looking out at the hibiscus in the garden when all of a sudden I

hear this zzz...zzzz...zzz...like snakes attacking through the leaves. I was only three years old but I'll never forget it. Then...Crash! Wham! So I get up and creep out into the livingroom. **Jesús**, what a mess! There were Zapata's peasants climbing in the windows trying to hide from the soldiers of Venustiano Carranza. They were all over the place with their guns...one guy lying in the middle of the carpet, all bloody and screaming like they were torturing him, his leg all smashed to a pulp. We could never get the red stain out of the carpet after that. We lived with it for years after...that splash of bright red blood!

FRIDA cackles gleefully.

Diego had to stop talking for a bit! That was the night I realized he likes me to play his little Indian. *(Putting flowers in her hair)* He loves it when I wear my Tehuana dresses. **Jo!** I stopped traffic just walking down the street...and the long skirts covered my gammy leg! I put rings on all my fingers and as much pre-Columbian jewellery as I could worm out of Diego's precious collection. Vogue magazine put me on the cover!

> *Frida suffers a tremendous spasm of pain. She begins to sing to try to mask the agony but can barely get the words out. As she sings, she puts on bracelets and rings on all her fingers.*

(Sings) **Voy a cantar un corrido
de esos que hacen padecer
y les suplico señores
me perdonen por favor.**

**Desde que los españoles
vinieron a este lugar
quedamos esclavizados
sin tener tierra ni hogar.**

Three photo flashes. FRIDA assumes poses after Nicolas Muray photographs.

'Art is like ham,' Diego told everyone. 'It nourishes people!' They loved him...what he said, what he painted, what he was.

Pause

They loved me, too. They did, you know, they really did. They loved me because I was with him.

Pause

Gringolandia! God, I hated it! Posh houses, fancy cars...yet everywhere you went there were men and women lined up for one piece of bread or some place to sleep. Nothing made sense there. They put their own communists in jail and then pay Diego to paint revolution on their buildings!

Night after night it's the same thing. I am in some terrible danger, all alone in the middle of a big open field. There is a little airplane there, just big enough for me but I don't know the first thing about how to fly it. I climb in and turn on the engine. Very slowly the propellor starts to rev up. The wheels lift off the ground. I can feel the wind on my face. I am in the air...I am flying and it's so goddamn easy! I don't need these useless ugly legs. I am flying free of my body...free of the earth...free at last of everything! I am more than just an ordinary woman...more than a man. I am complete...the very essence of myself. I know all the mysteries of the universe. I am the universe!

(Doubling over with pain) **Cabrona, es de la chingada aguantarte!**

That's what I've always wanted, even as a kid. One Christmas I begged my parents for an airplane. But the only thing for me under the tree was a pair of straw wings, the kind the Indians make in the villages. I was heart-broken...until my father convinced me if I really wanted to fly badly enough, nothing would stop me. 'You can be free as a bird', he said. And I believed him. I climbed a tree, closed my eyes, held my breath...and jumped!

> *FRIDA gives a jump and falls to the ground. The voice of GUILLERMO KAHLO echoes around the set while a piano plays a simple German melody.*

FATHER (off)

Lass nicht dich halten. Alles was du vorstellen. Kansst das kansst du machen das kannst du sein.

Whatever I could imagine! I drew an enormous circle...a gigantic "O" like a magic doorway...and I ran right through it. Down, down I ran...right down to the very centre of the earth.

Everything is golden...and so incredibly beautiful. And there is a little person here waiting for me! A little girl of my own age. I've never seen anyone so pretty ...and so, so happy. She's laughing and dancing all the time. I never tell anyone about her—she's my very own secret. I go down and see her whenever I'm lonely. She is more than my friend. She's who I've decided to be.

Pause

I don't know if Papa knows about her. I think he probably does. Papa is different from everyone else—that's what I love most about him.

FRIDA lifts herself into her wheelchair.

We walk down the street hand in hand and he

tells me things—why the light falls a certain way or why one bird has brighter feathers than another. Suddenly, he stops dead in his tracks, his lips almost smiling, his eyes fixed on one spot. For one moment it's like the whole world is standing still...waiting. Then, without any warning, he falls down in a heap frothing at the mouth. *(Angrily)* **Fuera...no es ningún espectáculo!** And take your hands off that camera! Take a deep breath, **Papaito.** Don't try to move yet. I'm here with you...everything's gonna be all right. I'm here with you...everything's gonna be all right.

Pause

One day, I got a horrible pain in my leg. I'm having a fit... just like Papa! But my leg is completely paralyzed. Polio, they call it. Poliomylitis. I'm scared I'm going to die. But I don't. I keep right on living...a cute little six-year-old cripple!

My father knew what I was feeling. He's the only one who ever understood me. I was his favourite...his **Frida, liebe Frida**. We'd catch butterflies and insects together and then dissect them under his microscope. 'You see, Frida, every single little thing is important. Even the teeniest little thing has it's place. It's all part of what we are!'

I think a lot about that. Especially on my bad days when I feel like hell and my painting seems a pile of shit. My little paintings!

Pause

Papa taught me so many things. I think he probably taught me everything he knew. I remember one day he said there was nothing completely black in the world. *(Smiling fondly, FRIDA makes gentle fun of her father's accent.)* 'In reality, the colour black does not exist, Frida. Always remember that.'

She laughs ruefully.

I don't know if I believe that! Red certainly exists. And blue—pure, electric. And all the pigments of the earth—the stain of the soil, the dark chocolate brown you can almost taste in **mole**, the faded smudge of a dying leaf—so different from the green of a leaf alive. I think the whole of Germany is that colour green—detached, scientific, inexorably sad!

Pause

Papa loved this country. It hurt him so much when people thought he didn't belong here. Then he would withdraw and he would hardly speak at all.

After a while he seemed to withdraw more and more.

Sometimes I can't even remember now what he looked like. That's why I painted him. So he'd never disappear altogether.

She wheels over to a stack of canvases and rifles through them until she finds the one of her family. Putting it on the easel, she points out the various family members as she speaks of them.

Everyone thought he was German but Jakob Kahlo and Henriette Kaufmann were really Hungarian Jews. They settled in Germany just before my father was born. Wilhelm they called him. He was very clever but one day he slipped and hit his head...and his whole world turned upside down! He started having fits. When his mother died and his father got married again, Wilhelm came as far away as he could...to Mexico. And just like that, he became Guillermo Kahlo!

An immigrant without money. A Mister Nobody, that's what Wilhelm was when he first came here! He did odd jobs...he even got married. But that same bad luck hung over him like he was cursed. His wife died having their second child! That's when he married my mother.

Dark little Matilde, all goody-goody, fresh out of the convent and the fair-skinned European Jew, a dyed-in-the-wool atheist! Right off the bat, Matilde convinces Guillermo he should have a profession.

So she gets hold of one of her father's cameras and they travel all over the country taking photographs, and before long my father is employed by the government as the first official photographer of Mexico's Cultural Heritage!

My parents produced four children—all girls. I was the third one. Then right after me came Cristina—my baby sister, Cristi, **la chaparrita**. That kid was very beautiful...

Pause

(Putting on her earrings) Though hardly anyone's ever been aware of my crippled leg...except Lupe, **claro.** She was out of her mind with jealousy when Diego and I got married. You remember Tina Modotti? Ah, she was really something...one hell of a photographer...she didn't give a damn what anybody thought about her. And she was gorgeous to boot! Though later on she turned against us. **Que tonteria!** Testifying Diego was a revisionist because he took capitalist money to pay for revolutionary murals! Anyway, before all that shit happened, Tina had a party for us at her place. Everybody was there—the **crème de la crème** of Mexico's political and cultural intelligentsia—all come to celebrate the wedding of the national hero to this unknown little box of tricks from Coyoacan...when in walks Lupe. I was a bit nervous when I saw her at first and I could tell Diego was too. But Lupe was **toda dulzura.** Only after a few shots of tequila

did she lift her skirt up to her waist to show her perfect legs. Then she reached down and lifted up my skirt, too. 'Look everybody, what Diego is settling for this time!'

I came home alone. After a few days Diego came to get me—it took him that long to sober up. He got roaring drunk after Lupe's little scene and he started firing his pistol at the record player, the windows, the plants, even at the guests! It was my first **indicio** of what it was going to be like to be the wife of the great Rivera!

Pause

Diego swears I'm a **bruja**, a regular little witch. He always marvels how I know when he's having an affair, even when he thinks he's being so sly and clever. But any woman worth her salt would know that. Deceit sets itself up like a game of chess. You look at the board after just a couple of moves and you know pretty well how it's all going to end.

But I was always a bit surprised Lupe actually showed her hand the way she did that night. By attacking me she made me **la víctima**...and she'd lived with Diego long enough to know he's always on the side of **la víctima**. Trotsky, for instance...

Pause

My practical mother decided that, despite everything, this big banana Diego Rivera'd have enough money to take care of my hospital bills. My father, all he said was: 'My daughter's a devil and not much to look at but she's intelligent. If you want her you can have her, but don't say I didn't warn you.' How could Diego pass up an offer like that?

It was a lousy deal you got, baby! Though it's only a matter of time...nothing lasts forever. Trotsky knew that. I like to think that at the end he wasn't even surprised to see that ice-pick coming at him.

When they killed him Diego went into hiding. I was all alone...I was very sick, I needed an operation. The police came and wrecked the whole studio and then they interrogated me for twelve hours. I didn't even know where Diego was...or why he left. He was afraid they would think it was him...but that didn't make sense. Trostsky was our friend...or had been...our guest.

It was Diego who brought him here. When they threw Trotsky out of Norway, he convinced the president to give him political asylum here in Mexico.

Trotsky and I spoke English together...a language his wife did not understand one word of!

She laughs and lights a cigarette.

Mind you, he was a bit old-fashioned. He couldn't stand for anyone to smoke in the same room and he was convinced women should not smoke at all.

But you were aware of the passion in him...and an anxiety, too, as if he could sense that time was running out. You comfort a man like that any way you can.

There is nothing as attractive as a man who wants to change the world...can you understand that? After all those cold northern countries surrounded by spies, and people everywhere trying to do him in, the colour and the warmth of Mexico was just what

Trotsky needed. At least in the beginning...

> *FRIDA picks up the watermelon and the knife.*

Still, I can't shake the feeling that by bringing Trotsky here we led him into a trap.

> *FRIDA gets out of her chair and performs a solemn dance to ancient Aztec music. In a ceremonious gesture, she cuts the melon open revealing a bleeding heart inside which stains her petticoat.*

Oops, a little accident!...and I gotta wear this!

I've been having accidents all my life. That's what they called the abortion I had here in Mexico. I was three months gone that time and the doctors said I'd never be able to carry a baby to term—the accident years ago had done things inside me that made it impossible. But in the States they said there was no reason I couldn't have a kid. I'd need a caesarian but that's no big deal.

It was hard to decide. I kept wondering if the...this

thing in my blood...this curse from my father...if I was gonna pass that along to the baby. And Diego was not crazy about the idea. He already had two kids with Lupe and another one years before with some Russian woman. And he has his work... that's all he really needs! But more than anything in the world I wanted my own little **Dieguito**!

Pause

It was hot as hell that summer in Detroit. On the fourth of July I don't think anybody stays at home... people are singing and dancing in the streets all night. It makes me homesick.

FRIDA is overtaken by pain.

Dios mio! I'm being torn apart! It is exactly the same as all those years ago...

Sound of a trolley car.

The sky is grey and dark. Alex and I catch a bus to come back home. It's a brand new bus with benches along either side—I can smell the wood and the fresh paint. It's been raining all day and we hardly get on it's so crowded. My pretty little Japanese parasol is all dripping and I have to hold it away so it won't wet my clothes. How slowly we're moving...but at last we are at the San Juan market. In front of us I can see a trolley car turning the corner.

The sound of the trolley grows louder.

I watch it coming toward us directly in front of the little Virgin of Guadalupe the bus driver has hanging on his rear-view mirror. The trolley and the little virgin seem to be dancing together...swaying together from side to side in slow motion. I watch her dancing as the trolley turns the corner and slams us up against the...aaaahhhh!

Sound of a collision.

Mira, la pobre bailarina. Mírala, está muerta!

I am the **bailarina** now...covered in gold! Someone on the bus had been carrying a package of gold powder and it sprinkled all over me and stuck to the blood.

An iron rod...

one of the hand-rails from the bus...
pierced right through me...
from my hip to my vagina!
A man picks me up in his arms and lays me on a billiard table right there on the street in front of a bar. He says they will have to remove the rod. But no-one wants to touch it so he does it himself.

I don't know who he was but he just put his knee on me and pulled. I remember his eyes looking at me as if he was forcing his will on me.

My whole body is crushed...my spine broken in three places.

That's when I first see you, **Pelona.**

MOVEMENT THREE

There is another knock at the door, more insistent this time.

MALE SERVANT (off)

Señorita Frida, estás bien? Te están esperando. Es muy tarde.

FRIDA

Jijo! Por qué tanta prisa? Chinga tu madre! Ya voy. Ya voy.

*The crazy crackling laughter of a dummy in a fun fair reverberates over the set. From inside the wardrobe we hear Frida and Cristi as children singing the **corrido**.*

The wardrobe glides to cover the doorway. Now, in place of the mirror on the wall, a surreal drawing is revealed depicting an eye, a clock, a severed leg and breasts spurting milk.

FRIDA backs away in horror as children's voices taunt her calling **"Frida, pata de palo"**. *Then she hears an echo of her father's voice coming from the easel. The mocking laughter sounds even louder and FRIDA turns to the skeleton on the wall.*

**Zorra! Cómo te atreves?
Calla. Calla. Calla te digo. Cállate!**

FRIDA furiously thrashes the vase of arum lilies which scatter on the floor. Finally the crazy laughter subsides. Grabbing the skeleton, she clutches it to her.

We ought to learn to be gentler with each other... we've been through so much together! You were with me again that night in Detroit. You remember what it was like...by morning there was nothing left inside me. Just the bright red clots all over the bed. I knew then I'd never have a baby. I would always be alone! There'll only ever be me...and you!

Pause

I couldn't bear gringo life anymore. We came home. But Diego had lost all faith in Mexico. He swore he'd never paint again. He hardly even wanted to eat.

I'd take him his lunch to the studio...Lupe taught me to do that...putting little surprises in it for him—those enchiladas he likes...and chocolate truffles!

Pause

At first I think there's no one there. He is not talking and he talks all the time. But he is there all right... beside his easel. The white lilies all over the floor look like they're spilling out of the canvas. They almost cover my sister Cristi. My beautiful baby sister! She is kneeling down, bent over, her long black hair hiding her face, and Diego is behind her, fucking her like a dog. The only sounds are his grunts as he pushes in and out...they don't even hear me come in.

Pause

I've loved other men. I've loved women, too. When your body is stitched and marked like a road map the way mine is, women are often the only reliable navigators. But they've all known I belong to Diego...that he'll always come first with me.

Ay, mi Diego! I don't know why I call him mine. He never will be mine...or anyone elses.

Fifteen years ago he told me he wanted a divorce. I thought he was joking. Being married never stopped him doing anything he wanted. But he insisted. 'I'm getting old and Frida's young and beautiful. She'll be better off without me.'

El Pendejo! He'd found out about my affair with Trotsky. Trotsky and my success in Paris were just too much for my **Dieguito.**

*The skeleton still in her arms,
FRIDA drags herself over to
her wheelchair.*

I know what he's like...but I know myself, too. I know what I need out of life, though God only knows for how much longer. **Mis doctorcitos... esos jijos médicos míos...**they love me madly...

they use my body like their own private playground! Bone transplants, bone removals. Now they say they're gonna amputate—cut off the whole damn leg. Ah —what the hell! I might as well go the whole hog *(Picking up the bottle of brandy and holding it aloft)* Peg-leg Frida, the great gammy queen herself!

Pause

I wish I was tall and strong like an Amazon. Size is important in how people see you. Think of the CIA and the Yankee marines and what they do to little governments they don't like. If a country's big you can't just go in and squash it like that...at least, not so easily. People, too, are harder to destroy when they're big. Like Diego. Everything's big about him —his body, his painting, his desire to live...

> *FRIDA suffers another spasm of pain. With difficulty she manages to wheel herself to her medicines where she prepares a syringe. Lifting up her skirt she injects it into her thigh.*

Diego? I gotta leave. It's getting late. Diego'll be waiting for me at the gallery. He says everybody's gonna be there and I gotta look my best...like a real pretty little **Mejicana**.

> *Getting out of her wheelchair FRIDA sits the skeleton in her place. Taking a flower from her hair, she sticks it in the skeleton's eye. Then she opens the wardrobe where an embroidered Tehuana dress is hanging. FRIDA puts on the dress. This is the last step in her ceremony and she must take her time.*

(Muttering as she puts on her skirt) **Al menos,** this'll hide the stains. No one'll know what the hell's under here!

They'll all be there with their goddamn cameras and their notebooks trying to work out if I'm alive or dead, wondering what Diego sees in me...why he's stayed with me all these years.

> *FRIDA, fully dressed at last, moves downstage and addresses the audience.*

When Diego divorced me I painted the two Fridas...the Mexican Frida he loved and the other

Frida inside me he couldn't seem to love at all. I wanted to tear the heart out of that Frida Diego didn't want. I tried to...God knows I tried every way I could to kill her off. But she wouldn't die. She kept right on there inside me, yelling her obscene truths, demanding to be heard! She's the one suffers inside me. Without her I don't exist at all. It's her life I paint.

> *The wardrobe glides again to its initial position freeing the doorway.*

There's so much to understand. So many things to find the colours for, the exact texture—the dust on a strand of hair...the tears that have not even begun to fall...the secrets hiding in the eyes.

> *FRIDA wheels the skeleton in the chair into position at her dressing table. Then with great dignity she hobbles to the doors up centre and flings them open.*

Ya estoy.

As celebratory Mexican music is heard FRIDA turns from the doorway and considers the surreal elements around the room —the death figures, the bleeding heart of the melon, the broken vase, the lilies and the wardrobe.

I've often wondered if my life had been different...y'know—happy...would I ever have painted at all?

FRIDA exits.

THE END

PLAYWRIGHT'S NOTE

The duality in Frida makes her an artist you must explore: Chilean painter Roser Bru was categoric when she first talked to me about Frida Kahlo. Although it is difficult to believe now, at that time Frida was hardly known outside Mexico, but the duality Roser spoke about fascinated me. She was referring especially to the fact that Frida, so determinedly a child of the New World, felt inextricably linked to Europe through the German Jewish father she adored. Roser who, as a teenager had been exiled with her family to Chile at the end of the Spanish Civil War, was well aware of the conflict such a dichotomy provokes and she knew that I, too, had grown up with many of the same tensions.

As I learned more about Frida I found her dualities to be manifold: the extraordinary beauty imposed on the deformed body; the tremendous vitality that withstood the constant pain and operations; the brutal honesty that made itself felt even when she resorted to duplicity to get what she wanted; the overt sexual duality that refused to recognize limits; the intelligence and courage which, at the very moment her life seemed to have been cut down, were to determine the icon she would become.

Frida—who lived intensely the political and artistic revolutions that shaped the 20th century—is truly a woman of our time. It seemed inevitable that, when I decided to give my daughter, actor Allegra Fulton, a very special gift, I should choose Frida Kahlo as the subject of the play I would write for her.

Vulnerable and provocative, Frida is a classic modern heroine. The myth she fabricated out of the tragedy of her life holds its own beside those of Medea, Antigone and Electra of ancient times.

Gloria Montero

Printed in Great Britain
by Amazon